ARKANSAS

The Natural State

BY
JOHN HAMILTON

Abdo & Daughters

An imprint of Abdo Publishing | abdopublishing.com

abdopublishing.com

Published by ABDO Publishing, a division of ABDO, PO Box 398166, Minneapolis, Minnesota 55439. Copyright © 2017 by Abdo Consulting Group, Inc. International copyrights reserved in all countries. No part of this book may be reproduced in any form without written permission from the publisher. ABDO & Daughters™ is a trademark and logo of ABDO Publishing.

Printed in the United States of America, North Mankato, Minnesota.
012016
092016

THIS BOOK CONTAINS
RECYCLED MATERIALS

Editor: Sue Hamilton   **Contributing Editor:** Bridget O'Brien
Graphic Design: Sue Hamilton
Cover Art Direction: Candice Keimig   **Cover Photo Selection:** Neil Klinepier
Cover Photo: iStock
Interior Images: Alamy, AP, Arkansas Historical Commission, Arkansas Secretary of State, Arkansas State Parks, Arkansas Travelers, City of Fayetteville, Corbis, Debbie Sikes, Granger, Gunter Küchler, Indians of Arkansas, iStock Photo, Library of Congress, Mile High Maps, Minden, Mountain High Maps, National Park Service, Northwest Arkansas Naturals, One Mile Up, U.S. Federal Government, U.S. Fish and Wildlife Service/Hagerty Ryan, University of Arkansas-Razorbacks, Walmart, Wark Photography, Wikimedia.

Statistics: *State and City Populations*, U.S. Census Bureau, July 1, 2014 estimates; *Land and Water Area*, U.S. Census Bureau, 2010 Census, MAF/TIGER database; *State Temperature Extremes*, NOAA National Climatic Data Center; *Climatology and Average Annual Precipitation*, NOAA National Climatic Data Center, 1980-2015 statewide averages; *State Highest and Lowest Points*, NOAA National Geodetic Survey.

Websites: To learn more about the United States, visit booklinks.abdopublishing.com. These links are routinely monitored and updated to provide the most current information available.

Cataloging-in-Publication Data

Names: Hamilton, John, 1959- author.
Title: Arkansas / by John Hamilton.
Description: Minneapolis, MN : Abdo Publishing, [2016] | The United States of America | Includes index.
Identifiers: LCCN 2015957487 | ISBN 9781680783063 (print) | ISBN 9781680774108 (ebook)
Subjects: LCSH: Arkansas--Juvenile literature.
Classification: DDC 976.7--dc23
LC record available at http://lccn.loc.gov/2015957487

CONTENTS

The Natural State. 4

Quick Facts 6

Geography. 8

Climate and Weather 12

Plants and Animals. 14

History. 18

Did You Know? 24

People 26

Cities 30

Transportation 34

Natural Resources. 36

Industry 38

Sports. 40

Entertainment 42

Timeline. 44

Glossary 46

Index 48

THE NATURAL STATE

Arkansas is called "The Natural State." Fertile fields of cotton and rice in the south stretch to the horizon. The Ozark and Ouachita Mountains in the north and west reach to the sky. Forests cover half the state. Networks of caves wind their way deep under the Earth. Arkansas even has a working diamond mine!

Most important are Arkansas's people. Whether they come from the hustle and bustle of big-city streets, or the more laid-back countryside, Arkansans have a reputation for being friendly and high spirited. They love Creole, catfish, and Southern BBQ recipes, but they're just as likely to be found enjoying French cuisine in a ritzy Little Rock restaurant. Folk crafts, banjo music, and corn bread coexist with kayaks, Walmart, and presidential politics.

Ozark Mountains

Arkansas's famous Old Mill is a replica of an 1880s water-powered grist mill.

QUICK FACTS

Name: The word Arkansas comes from a Quapaw Native American word meaning either "Land of the Downriver People" or "People of the South Wind."

State Capital: Little Rock, population 197,706

Date of Statehood: June 15, 1836 (25th state)

Population: 2,966,369 (32nd-most populous state)

Area (Total Land and Water): 53,179 square miles (137,733 sq km), 29th-largest state

Largest City: Little Rock, population 197,706

Nickname: The Natural State, the Land of Opportunity, the Razorback State

Motto: *Regnat populus* (The people rule)

State Bird: Mockingbird

State Flower: Apple Blossom

State Rock: Bauxite

State Mineral: Quartz

State Tree: Pine

State Songs: "Arkansas (You Run Deep in Me)" and "Oh, Arkansas"

Highest Point: Mount Magazine, 2,753 feet (839 m)

Lowest Point: Ouachita River, 55 feet (17 m)

Average July High Temperature: 91°F (33°C)

Record High Temperature: 120°F (49°C), in Ozark, August 10, 1936

Average January Low Temperature: 30°F (-1°C)

Record Low Temperature: -29°F (-34°C), in Gravette, February 13, 1905

Average Annual Precipitation: 51 inches (130 cm)

Number of U.S. Senators: 2

Number of U.S. Representatives: 4

U.S. Presidents Born in Arkansas: William Jefferson Clinton

U.S. Postal Service Abbreviation: AR

GEOGRAPHY

Arkansas is part of the American South. It is the 29th-largest state, covering 53,179 square miles (137,733 sq km). The Interior Highlands region is in the northern and western parts of the state. It combines two mountainous areas: the Ozark Plateau and the Ouachita (pronounced "WAH-shi-tah") Mountains.

The Ozarks are a gently rolling series of forested mountains. Rivers cut through the sedimentary rocks, creating deep valleys, waterfalls, and caves. The rugged Boston Mountains are part of the Ozarks.

Just south of the Ozark Plateau are the Ouachita Mountains. The state's highest peak, Mount Magazine, is found here. It rises 2,753 feet (839 m) above sea level.

The Ozark Mountains are among the oldest mountain ranges on Earth.

Arkansas's total land and water area is 53,179 square miles (137,733 sq km). It is the 29th-largest state. The state capital is Little Rock.

Arkansas's other major region is called the Lowlands. It occupies the southern and eastern parts of the state. In the east is the Mississippi Alluvial Plain. It is often simply called the Delta. It follows the meandering north-south path of the Mississippi River, which forms most of Arkansas's eastern border. Alluvial means *stream-deposited*. This flat, fertile area was built up over millions of years by rivers overflowing their banks and depositing thick layers of soil, perfect for farming. The land is flat except for a narrow group of gently rising hills called Crowley's Ridge, which runs north and south.

The Mississippi River divides Arkansas (left) and the state of Mississippi (right). This low-lying river Delta region is an excellent area for farming.

The Grand Prairie is in the southeast part of the state. It once held almost one million acres (404,686 ha) of native tallgrass prairie. Today, many rice farms are found in the region.

Important rivers that flow through Arkansas include the Arkansas, White, Red, St. Francis, and Ouachita

The 40-mile-long (64-km) Lake Ouachita is the largest lake located completely within Arkansas.

Rivers, all of which empty into the Mississippi River. Lake Ouachita is the largest body of water in Arkansas. It is a reservoir formed by a large hydroelectric dam built on the Ouachita River. It is a popular place to camp, fish, and scuba dive. The largest natural body of water in the state is Lake Chicot, an oxbow lake near the Mississippi River in the southeast corner of Arkansas.

CLIMATE AND
WEATHER

A severe thunderstorm hits rural Arkansas at sunset.

Arkansas has a "humid subtropical" climate. Summers are warm and humid. Winters are mild. The southern Lowlands get a lot of hot days in late summer, and more rain than in the north. Hurricanes and tropical storms sometimes reach Arkansas after passing through Louisiana or Mississippi.

The northern and western Highlands have a more moderate climate than the south. Summers are hot, but less humid. In winter, temperatures often dip below freezing. Snow is not unusual.

The statewide average high temperature in July is 91°F (33°C). The record high temperature is 120°F (49°C), which happened on August 10, 1936, in the town of Ozark. The average low temperature in January is 30°F (-1°C). During a cold snap on February 13, 1905, the town of Gravette recorded the state's record cold temperature of -29°F (-34°C). The statewide rainfall average in Arkansas is 51 inches (130 cm).

A worker stays hydrated as summer temperatures soar in Little Rock, Arkansas.

Winter snow causes slippery conditions in Little Rock.

Arkansas natives are used to hot, humid summers and mild, but sometimes snowy winters. Weather systems from surrounding states often converge on Arkansas, resulting in severe, stormy conditions.

CLIMATE AND WEATHER

PLANTS AND ANIMALS

Elk

Arkansas used to be called "The Bear State" because its woodlands were filled with black bears. Years of overhunting almost exterminated them. Thanks to new hunting regulations and restocking, black bears can now be found in the Ozark and Ouachita Mountains. Elk have also been reintroduced in northern Arkansas.

White-tailed deer are Arkansas's official state mammal. Other common mammals include squirrels, rabbits, beavers, opossums, minks, weasels, raccoons, muskrats, armadillos, striped skunks, feral hogs, gray and red foxes, and river otters. There are several species of bats in Arkansas. Three are endangered, including the gray bat, the Indiana bat, and the Ozark big-eared bat.

Gray Bats

Diana fritillary

The official state insect of Arkansas is the honeybee. The state butterfly is the Diana fritillary. There are more than 400 species of birds that live in Arkansas. They include wild turkeys, bald eagles, red-tailed hawks, great horned owls, ruby-throated hummingbirds, endangered red-cockaded woodpeckers, wood ducks, egrets, turkey vultures, and many others. The mockingbird is the state bird.

Wild Turkey

The rivers and lakes of Arkansas are teeming with 233 species of fish. They include bass, catfish, carp, bluegill, trout, bullhead, gar, pickerel, sunfish, and walleye. The strange Ozark cavefish has no eyes. It spends its life in the sunless streams that flow through Arkansas's limestone caverns. It is a threatened species that may someday become extinct. Another odd species is the paddlefish. Found swimming in larger waterways such as the Arkansas and Ouachita Rivers, it has a snout that resembles a canoe paddle.

A fishing guide holds up a brown trout caught in Arkansas's White River.

Paddlefish

Arkansas has more than 600 species of native wildflowers.

There are more than 600 species of native wildflowers growing in Arkansas. They splash secluded meadows and roadsides with bursts of color. They include black-eyed Susan, ox-eye daisy, butterfly weed, goldenrod, Indian paintbrush, Queen Anne's lace, spider lily, and purple coneflower.

The official Arkansas state flower is the apple blossom. It has delicate pink and white petals. In the past, apples were one of the state's most important cash crops.

There are about 190 species of trees growing in Arkansas. Pine is the official state tree. Native to Arkansas are shortleaf and loblolly pine. There are a great many types of oak trees found in Arkansas forests. Other trees include elm, hickory, willow, magnolia, cottonwood, cypress, ash, and cork.

PLANTS AND ANIMALS

HISTORY

Long before Europeans settled in North America, thousands of Native Americans lived in the land that is today called Arkansas. They included people from the Caddo, Osage, and Quapaw tribes.

In 1541, Spanish explorer Hernando de Soto arrived with an army of more than 600 conquistadors. They were seeking gold and other treasure. They explored much of the new land, but found no gold.

On June 28, 1541, Spanish explorer Hernando de Soto and his army crossed the Mississippi River and arrived in the land that is today called Arkansas.

Father Jacques Marquette and fur trader Louis Jolliet traveled down the Mississippi River by canoe, arriving in Arkansas in 1673.

More than 100 years after de Soto's expedition, Father Jacques Marquette, a French missionary, and French-Canadian explorer and fur trader Louis Jolliet, explored the area. They traveled by canoe down the Mississippi River and arrived in Arkansas in 1673. Shortly afterward, in 1682, another Frenchman traveled to Arkansas. René-Robert Cavelier, Sieur de La Salle led an expedition to expand the French fur trade. He declared a huge section of the continent along the Mississippi River Valley, including today's Arkansas, to be French territory. He named the new territory Louisiana, in honor of French King Louis XIV.

Around this time, French explorers gave Arkansas its name. It was taken from a Native American term that means "people who live downstream," referring to the Quapaw tribe.

An aerial view of the Arkansas Post National Memorial, with the Arkansas River in the background. This area held the first semi-permanent French trading post known as "Poste de Arkansea." It was established by Henri de Tonti in 1686.

The first European settlement in Arkansas was a French trading post. It was built in 1686 near a Quapaw Native American village. Today, the site is preserved as the Arkansas Post National Memorial. It is near the town of Gillett.

French fur trappers worked in Arkansas for many years, but the land was too remote to attract many settlers. The European superpowers of France, Great Britain, and Spain fought long wars in the 18th century. Louisiana Territory, including Arkansas, changed hands several times. In 1803, French ruler Napoleon Bonaparte sold the vast territory to the United States as part of the Louisiana Purchase. The sale nearly doubled the young nation's land area.

Arkansas became a United States territory in 1819. Controversy erupted over whether to allow slavery in Arkansas. The pro-slavery side won. Cotton was an important cash crop, and landowners wanted slave workers. Arkansas became a state on June 15, 1836.

In 1860, newly elected President Abraham Lincoln vowed to restrict slavery. Cheap slave labor made farming in the South very profitable. Southern slave states, including Arkansas, seceded (withdrew) from the United States, igniting the Civil War in 1861.

Several Civil War battles took place in Arkansas. The state was important because it controlled boat traffic along the Mississippi River. In 1865, Northern forces won the war and put an end to slavery. Arkansas rejoined the Union in 1868.

In 1862, Confederate troops fought the Union army in Arkansas at the Battle of Pea Ridge. Union forces won this deadly Civil War battle.

Rebuilding war-torn Arkansas was difficult. By the 1870s, railroad companies laid hundreds of miles of tracks that crisscrossed the state. This made it much easier to move goods and people. Slowly, the Civil War's scars began to heal.

The war's legacy of racial hatred proved much harder to repair. Freed slaves, along with poor whites, were often mistreated. Segregation, the separation of blacks and whites in everyday settings, was common. Many African Americans left Arkansas to find better jobs and schools in Northern states.

White segregationists in Little Rock, Arkansas, protest the admission of African Americans to their all-white schools in the 1950s.

In 1957, the teenagers known as the "Little Rock Nine" were the first African American students to attend Central High School in Little Rock, Arkansas. To protect them, U.S. Army troops often accompanied the black teens at school.

In 1954, the U.S. Supreme Court ruled against segregated schools. In 1957, a federal court ordered all-white schools in the capital of Little Rock to enroll African American children.

Nine black students, called the "Little Rock Nine," bravely tried to attend class at all-white Central High School. President Dwight Eisenhower sent 1,000 U.S. Army troops to stop riots and safely escort the black students to class. Within two years, all four high schools in Little Rock were integrated. The story of the Little Rock Nine brought attention to the civil rights movement. Whites and blacks today learn and work together throughout Arkansas. Racial attitudes have changed, and so have economic opportunities.

There are many new science and technology companies in the state, as well as retail giants such as Walmart. People today come to Arkansas seeking a much brighter future.

DID YOU KNOW?

Crater of Diamonds State Park

Bobbie Oskarson holds an 8.52-carat diamond she found at Arkansas's Crater of Diamonds State Park in June 2015.

- Millions of years ago, diamonds formed deep underneath Arkansas and were brought to the surface by a violent volcanic eruption. Today, Crater of Diamonds State Park, near Murfreesboro, is the only public diamond mine in the world. It is a place where anyone can pay a small fee and hunt for precious gems. The park rules say "finders keepers," no matter how big a diamond someone unearths. The largest diamond ever found in North America, the Uncle Sam Diamond, came from Arkansas. Discovered in 1924, it was a 40-carat white diamond.

- The area known today as Hot Springs National Park was set aside by Congress in 1832. This was 40 years before America's first national park, Yellowstone, was established. With an average temperature of 143°F (62°C), the healing baths have long been used by patients with arthritis and other ailments.

- In the rural back roads of the Ozark Mountains, near the town of Dover, mysterious lights are often reported flickering low in the sky. Since they were first spotted in the late 1800s, nobody has yet explained the legend of the Dover Lights. Some believe they are the ghosts of Spanish conquistadors from the 1500s, still searching for gold and other treasure.

PEOPLE

William Jefferson Clinton (1946-) was the 42nd president of the United States, serving from 1993 to 2001. He was born in Hope, Arkansas, but grew up in Hot Springs. He served as the governor of Arkansas from 1979 to 1981, and from 1983 to 1992.

As president, Clinton pushed for education reform and economic development. The economy thrived under his leadership, but his presidency was also marred by controversy. Accused of lying to Congress, Clinton became only the second president to ever be impeached by the U.S. House of Representatives. The Senate, however, did not convict him. Clinton finished his second term with the highest public approval rating of any president since World War II.

Hillary Rodham Clinton (1947-) was active in politics and public service as a young woman. She married future President Bill Clinton in 1975. They met while both earned law degrees from Yale University. She spent 12 years in Arkansas as First Lady when Bill Clinton was governor of the state. She also taught law and worked at a Little Rock law firm. During Bill Clinton's presidency, she served as the nation's First Lady in Washington, DC, from 1993 to 2001. She won election as a U.S. Senator from New York in 2000, serving from 2001 to 2009. She also served as President Barack Obama's Secretary of State from 2009 to 2013. In 2016, she became the first woman to run for president as a major political party candidate (Democrat).

Hattie Caraway (1878-1950) was the first woman elected to the United States Senate. Her husband, Arkansas Senator Thaddeus Caraway, died in 1931 while in office, so she took his place. In 1932, the people of Arkansas sent Hattie back to Washington, DC. She won another election after that, serving in the Senate until 1945. Caraway was born in Tennessee, but moved to Arkansas after she married.

Bass Reeves (1838-1910) was a legendary deputy U.S. marshal and one of the first African American lawmen west of the Mississippi River. He won fame for his toughness and ability to catch even the most hardened criminals. Reeves was born a slave in Crawford County, Arkansas, in 1838. During the Civil War, he escaped to Indian Territory (modern-day Oklahoma), where he lived with Creek and Seminole Native Americans. In 1875, he became a deputy U.S. marshal. He was one of the greatest gunfighters of the Old West, able to shoot a pistol or rifle with either hand. He worked for 32 years in Indian Territory, and claimed that he captured more than 3,000 outlaws.

Jay Hanna "Dizzy" Dean (1910-1974) was a Major League Baseball pitcher in the 1930s and 1940s. Nicknamed "Dizzy" because of his colorful personality, he played most of his career for the St. Louis Cardinals and Chicago Cubs. In 1934, he won an incredible 30 games for the Cardinals. He was elected to the National Baseball Hall of Fame in 1953. Dean was born in Lucas, Arkansas.

Douglas MacArthur (1880-1964) was a U.S. Army five-star general. During World War II, he was the Supreme Commander of Allied Forces in the Pacific. With his trademark corncob pipe, he led America and its allies to victory over Japan in 1945. He later went on to command the United Nations forces that fought in the Korean War. MacArthur was born in Little Rock, Arkansas.

Johnny Cash (1932-2003) was a superstar of country, folk, rock, blues, and gospel music. His deep, rich voice and guitar playing helped him sell more than 90 million albums in a career that spanned nearly 50 years. Fan favorites included "I Walk the Line," "Ring of Fire," and "Folsom Prison Blues." Cash was born in Kingsland, Arkansas.

CITIES

Little Rock is the capital of Arkansas. It is also the largest city in the state, with a population of 197,706. Located near the center of Arkansas, Little Rock was founded in 1821. Its name comes from a landmark on the Arkansas River, which flows north of the city. French pioneers called the rock formation on the bank of the river *la petite roche*, which means "the little rock." The city is the economic and cultural center of Arkansas. It hosts many large corporations, as well as hospitals, orchestras, art galleries, and museums.

Fort Smith is the second-largest city in Arkansas. Its population is 87,351. The city is on the border of western Arkansas and Oklahoma. It was founded in 1817 where the Arkansas River meets the Poteau River. A regional manufacturing center, the city is home to many large corporations that create goods and services sold nationwide. In its early days, Fort Smith was a military post. It played an important roll in settling the Old West. The U.S. Marshals Museum is located in the city.

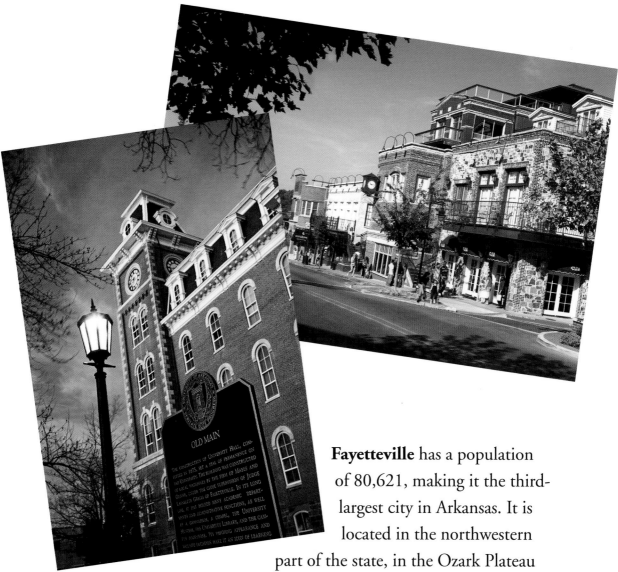

OLD MAIN

THE CONSTRUCTION OF UNIVERSITY HALL, COMPLETED IN 1875, SET A SEAL OF PERMANENCE ON THE UNIVERSITY. THE BUILDING WAS CONSTRUCTED OF LOCAL MATERIALS BY THE FIRM OF MAYES AND OLIVER, UNDER THE CLOSE SUPERVISION OF JUDGE LAFAYETTE GREGG OF FAYETTEVILLE. IN ITS LONG LIFE, IT HAS HOUSED MANY ACADEMIC DEPARTMENTS AND ADMINISTRATIVE FUNCTIONS, AS WELL AS A GYMNASIUM, A CHAPEL, THE UNIVERSITY MUSEUM, THE UNIVERSITY LIBRARY, AND THE CAMPUS BOOKSTORE. ITS IMPOSING APPEARANCE AND HILLTOP LOCATION MAKE IT AN ICON OF LEARNING

Fayetteville has a population of 80,621, making it the third-largest city in Arkansas. It is located in the northwestern part of the state, in the Ozark Plateau region. Founded in 1828, it is a very business-friendly city, with high employment rates. It is also a very popular place to retire. Fayetteville is home to the University of Arkansas, which was founded in 1871. When classes are in session, the "Razorbacks" give the city a very youthful, college-town atmosphere. There are plenty of sports, music, shopping, and learning opportunities.

Springdale has a population of 76,565. It is located just north of Fayetteville in the Ozark Plateau region. Founded in 1838, it is home to several industrial companies and a community college. Springdale is called "The Poultry Capital of the World," thanks to Tyson Foods, the city's largest employer.

Jonesboro has a population of 72,210. Located in the northeast part of Arkansas, it is a center for manufacturing, as well as education, retail business, and medicine. Agriculture is also important. Many large farms surround the city. Jonesboro is home to Arkansas State University, the second-largest university in the state.

TRANSPORTATION

Arkansas has a large state highway system. More than 16,000 miles (25,750 km) of roads link cities and ports to the entire nation. Interstate highways also connect the state's major cities.

Arkansas makes good use of its rivers to transport goods. Using barges is a low-cost way to move heavy items such as steel or grain. Along the Arkansas River are ports serving the cities of Fort Smith, Little Rock, and Pine Bluff. Ports along the Ouachita River include Camden and Crossett. Four additional ports are located along the west bank of the Mississippi River, including Helena, Osceola, West Memphis, and Yellow Bend.

A barge transports goods on the Arkansas River.

A member of a locomotive crew climbs up to the cab as Amtrak's Texas Eagle stops at the station in Little Rock, Arkansas. The passenger train runs daily from Chicago, Illinois, to San Antonio, Texas, making stops along the way.

The port at Little Rock has its own railroad, which handles more than 10,000 freight cars per year. It connects to the rest of Arkansas's extensive railway system, which includes about 2,750 miles (4,426 km) of track. In addition to more than two dozen railroads that haul freight across Arkansas, Amtrak's Texas Eagle shuttles passengers between several cities.

Six major airlines fly in and out of Bill and Hillary Clinton National Airport, located in Little Rock. Formerly known as Little Rock National Airport, it is the state's largest, serving more than 2.2 million passengers annually. Other major airports serve Bentonville, Fort Smith, and Texarkana. Smaller airports are found in Hot Springs, Fayetteville, Harrison, Pine Bluff, and Jonesboro.

NATURAL
RESOURCES

One of Arkansas's most valuable natural resources is its fertile soil. Nearly 50,000 farms are in Arkansas, stretching out across 6.2 million acres (2.5 million ha) of land used to grow crops. Another 8.3 million acres (3.4 million ha) are used to raise livestock.

Arkansas is the number one producer of rice in the United States. Soybeans, cotton, wheat, corn, poultry, and catfish are other important agricultural products.

Arkansas farmers grow rice on about 1.3 million acres (526,091 ha) each year. They contribute more than $6 billion to the state's economy each year.

A SECO Energy field manager checks a production well collecting and piping natural gas from black shale near Quitman, Arkansas.

A quartz crystal is found at Fiddler's Ridge Mine, near Mount Ida, Arkansas. Arkansas's crystals are some of the most beautiful in the world.

Arkansas has almost 19 million acres (7.7 million ha) of timberland, covering more than half the state. Oak, hickory, and pine trees are common. Southern yellow pine is a dense wood used in construction and flooring. Arkansas is the fifth-largest softwood producer in the country.

Natural gas is captured in the northern part of Arkansas, while oil is found in the far south. Mines and quarries statewide produce crushed stone, iron ore, coal, slate, bauxite, and vanadium. Most of the country's bromine supply comes from Arkansas. The state is famous for the purity of its quartz crystals. It is also the only state in the country with an active diamond mine.

INDUSTRY

The aerospace industry is especially strong in Arkansas. Several companies make commercial and military aircraft and parts. Dassault Falcon Jet Corporation specializes in private aircraft at its Little Rock facility.

The leading manufacturing industry in Arkansas is food products. These include bakery goods, meats, poultry, canned vegetables, and rice. Tyson Foods is the biggest poultry producer in the country. The company's headquarters is in Springdale.

The biotechnology industry is strong in Arkansas. Scientists explore new ways to make food safer and more nutritious. Major employers include Riceland Foods, Tyson Foods, and the Food and Drug Administration's National Center for Toxicological Research, near Pine Bluff.

Many of Dassault Falcon Jets's luxury business planes are built in Little Rock.

Sam Walton (1918-1992) founded Walmart stores in 1962. Its headquarters (below) is in Bentonville, Arkansas. The company is now the world's biggest discount retail chain.

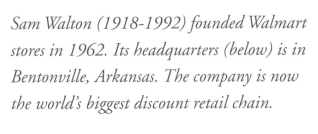

Arkansas factories make chemicals, electric motors, heating and cooling equipment, plastics, motor vehicle parts, and wood products. Dillard's is one of the country's top retail department store chains. Walmart is the world's biggest discount retail chain. Founded in 1962 by Sam Walton, the company today has more than 11,000 stores in 27 countries. Its headquarters is in Bentonville.

Tourism is a growing industry in Arkansas. In 2013, visitors spent almost $6 billion. More and more people are discovering all the scenery, shopping, food, museums, and historical sites the Natural State has to offer.

SPORTS

There are no major league sports teams in Arkansas. However, the state hosts two Minor League Baseball teams. The Arkansas Travelers are based in North Little Rock. The "Travs" are an affiliate of the Los Angeles Angels of Anaheim, California. Arkansas's second baseball team is the Northwest Arkansas Naturals. They began playing in Springdale in 2008, and are an affiliate of the Kansas City Royals.

Arkansans love playing and watching high school and college football. The University of Arkansas Razorbacks are hugely popular, not only in their hometown of Fayetteville, but statewide as well. The team became known as the Razorbacks in 1910 after football coach Hugo Bezdek said his team played "like a wild band of razorback hogs."

Outdoor sports are a way of life for Arkansans. The state has some of the best hunting and fishing in the country. Trout and bass are a favorite pursuit in the state's many rivers, streams, and reservoirs, such as Bull Shoals and Greers Ferry. Other activities include canoeing down the Buffalo National River, camping, bicycling, or simply stargazing on a clear Arkansas night.

ENTERTAINMENT

Music has always been an important part of Arkansas life. Blues and country are very popular, but other musical styles have eager fans as well. The Arkansas Symphony Orchestra has been playing in Little Rock since 1966. Other fine orchestras are found in Fort Smith, El Dorado, Fayetteville, Bentonville, and Texarkana. The King Biscuit Blues Festival is held annually in Helena. It is one of the largest outdoor blues festivals in the country.

Little Rock is the cultural center of Arkansas. In addition to its orchestra, it boasts an art museum, a botanical garden, and a zoo. Also located in Little Rock is the popular William J. Clinton Presidential Library & Museum.

Ozark Mountain Bluegrass Musicians

William J. Clinton Presidential Library & Museum

The Blanchard Springs Caverns is a living, changing cave. It is filled with nearly every type of calcite formation found in limestone caves.

Because of its water-eroded limestone, Arkansas has many caves. Blanchard Springs Caverns, near the town of Mountain View, is one of the most spectacular caves in the country.

There are hundreds of festivals held all around the state, especially in the summer. Food festivals celebrate peaches, grapes, tomatoes, watermelons, and purple hull peas. Others feature chili-cooking contests, giant barbecues, and catfish fries. Toad Suck Daze in the city of Conway features live bands, a parade, and toad races.

ENTERTAINMENT

TIMELINE

5000 BC—First humans arrive in Arkansas. They later group themselves into various Native American tribes.

1541—Hernando de Soto of Spain searches for gold in the Arkansas area.

1686—The first permanent settlement within the future state of Arkansas is built by the French.

1803—France sells Arkansas to the United States as part of the Louisiana Purchase.

1836—Arkansas becomes the 25th state to join the Union.

1861—The Civil War begins. Arkansas joins the Confederates in order to keep slavery legal.

1865—Arkansas and all other rebel Southern states are defeated. Slaves are freed.

1950s—The movement to give African Americans full equality gathers strength.

1957—Little Rock High School enrolls its first African American students.

1992—William Jefferson Clinton becomes the first Arkansas native elected president of the United States.

2002—Walmart becomes the world's largest corporation.

2004—William J. Clinton Presidential Library & Museum opens in November.

2009-2013—Hillary Rodham Clinton, the former First Lady of Arkansas, serves as the U.S. Secretary of State under President Barack Obama.

GLOSSARY

CIVIL RIGHTS MOVEMENT

A nationwide effort beginning in the 1950s to reform federal and state laws so that African Americans could enjoy full equality.

CIVIL WAR

The war fought between America's Northern and Southern states from 1861-1865. The Southern states were for slavery. They wanted to start their own country. Northern states fought against slavery and a division of the country.

CONQUISTADORS

Spanish military men, especially those who conquered the New World in the 1500s.

CREOLE

Food prepared with pepper and other heavy spices. Some popular Creole dishes are red beans and rice, jambalaya, and gumbo.

DELTA

A triangular-shaped section of land formed from sediments where the mouth of a river meets an ocean or other body of water. A delta can fan out over a distance of a few yards or many miles.

IMPEACH

To charge a government official with misconduct.

Louisiana Purchase

A purchase by the United States from France in 1803 of a huge section of land west of the Mississippi River. The United States nearly doubled in size after the purchase. The young country paid about $15 million for more than 820,000 square miles (2.1 million sq km) of land.

Oxbow Lake

A crescent-shaped lake. An oxbow lake forms when a section of a river is cut off by land, leaving the curved section of water in place to form a lake.

Plain

A large, flat area of land, often filled with grasses, but with few trees.

Plateau

A large area of land that is mainly flat but much higher than the land that neighbors it.

Secede

To withdraw membership in a union or alliance.

Segregationist

A person who believes that people of different races should not mix together.

Union

The Northern states united against the Confederacy. "Union" also refers to all of the states of the United States. President Lincoln wanted to preserve the Union, keeping the Northern and Southern states together.

Waterway

A stream or river wide and deep enough for boats to travel along.

INDEX

A

America 29
Amtrak 35
Anaheim, CA 40
Angels (baseball team) 40
Arkansas Post National Memorial 20
Arkansas River 11, 16, 30, 31, 34
Arkansas State University 33
Arkansas Symphony Orchestra 42
Arkansas Travelers 40
Army, U.S. 23, 29

B

Bear State, The 14
Bentonville, AR 35, 39, 42
Bezdek, Hugo 40
Bill and Hillary Clinton National Airport 35
Blanchard Springs Caverns 43
Bonaparte, Napoleon 20
Boston Mountains 8
Buffalo National River 41
Bull Shoals Lake 41

C

Caddo (tribe) 18
California 40
Camden, AR 34
Caraway, Hattie 27
Caraway, Thaddeus 27
Cardinals (baseball team) 28
Cash, Johnny 29
Central High School 23
Chicago, IL 28
Chicago Cubs 28
Chicot, Lake 11
Civil War 21, 22, 28
Clinton, Hillary Rodham 27
Clinton, William "Bill" Jefferson 26, 27
Congress, U.S. 25, 26
Conway, AR 43
Crater of Diamonds State Park 24
Crawford County 28
Crawley's Ridge 10
Creek (tribe) 28
Crossett, AR 34
Cubs (baseball team) 28

D

Dassault Falcon Jet Corporation 38
Dean, Jay Hanna "Dizzy" 28
Delta 10
Democrat 27
Dillard's 39
Dover, AR 25
Dover Lights 25

E

Earth 4
Eisenhower, Dwight 23
El Dorado, AR 42

F

Fayetteville, AR 32, 33, 35, 40, 42
First Lady 27
"Folsom Prison Blues" 29
Food and Drug Administration 38
Fort Smith, AR 31, 34, 35, 42
France 20

G

Gillett, AR 20
Grand Prairie 11
Gravette, AR 12
Great Britain 20
Greers Ferry Lake 41

H

Harrison, AR 35
Helena, AR 34, 42
Highlands 12
Hope, AR 26
Hot Springs, AR 26, 35
Hot Springs National Park 25
House of Representatives, U.S. 26

I

"I Walk The Line" 29
Indian Territory 28
Interior Highlands 8

J

Japan 29
Jolliet, Louis 19
Jonesboro, AR 33, 35

K

Kansas City Royals 40
King Biscuit Blues Festival 42
Kingsland, AR 29
Korean War 29

L

La Salle, René-Robert Cavelier, Sieur de 19
Lincoln, Abraham 21
Little Rock, AR 4, 23, 27, 29, 30, 34, 35, 38, 42
Little Rock National Airport 35
Little Rock Nine 23
Los Angeles Angels 40
Louis XIV, King 19
Louisiana (state) 12
Louisiana (territory) 19, 20
Louisiana Purchase 20
Lowlands (region) 10, 12
Lucas, AR 28

M

MacArthur, Douglas 29
Magazine, Mount 8
Major League Baseball 28
Marquette, Jacques 19
Minor League Baseball 40
Mississippi (state) 12
Mississippi Alluvial Plain 10
Mississippi River 10, 11, 19, 21, 28, 34
Mississippi River Valley 19
Mountain View, AR 43
Murfreesboro, AR 24

N

National Baseball Hall of Fame 28
National Center for Toxicological Research 38
Natural State, The 4, 39
New York 27
North America 18, 24
North Little Rock, AR 40
Northwest Arkansas Naturals 40

O

Obama, Barack 27
Oklahoma 28, 31
Old West 28, 31
Osage (tribe) 18
Osceola, AR 34
Ouachita, Lake 11
Ouachita Mountains 4, 8, 14
Ouachita River 11, 16, 34
Ozark, AR 12
Ozark Mountains 4, 8, 14, 25
Ozark Plateau 8, 32, 33

P

Pacific Ocean 29
Pine Bluff, AR 34, 35, 38
Poteau River 31
Poultry Capital of the World, The 33

Q

Quapaw (tribe) 18, 19, 20

R

Razorbacks 32, 40
Red River 11
Reeves, Bass 28
Riceland Foods 38
"Ring of Fire" 29
Royals (baseball team) 40

S

Secretary of State 27
Seminole (tribe) 28
Senate, U.S. 26, 27
Soto, Hernando de 18, 19
South 8, 21
Spain 20
Springdale, AR 33, 38, 40
St. Francis River 11
St. Louis, MO 28
St. Louis Cardinals 28
Supreme Commander of Allied Forces in the Pacific 29
Supreme Court, U.S. 23

T

Tennessee 27
Texarkana, AR 35, 42
Texas Eagle (train) 35
Toad Suck Daze 43
Travs (see Arkansas Travelers)
Tyson Foods 33, 38

U

Uncle Sam Diamond 24
Union 21
United Nations 29
United States 20, 21, 26, 27, 28, 29, 36
University of Arkansas 32, 40
U.S. Marshals Museum 31

W

Walmart 4, 23, 39
Walton, Sam 39
Washington, DC 27
West Memphis, AR 34
White River 11
William J. Clinton Presidential Library & Museum 42
World War II 26, 29

Y

Yale University 27
Yellow Bend, AR 34
Yellowstone National Park 25